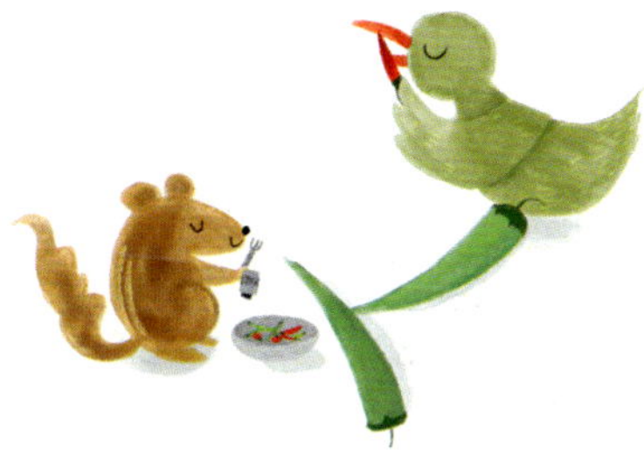

# A BOUNTY OF CHILLIES

By Niyatee Sharma

Illustrated by Vibha Surya

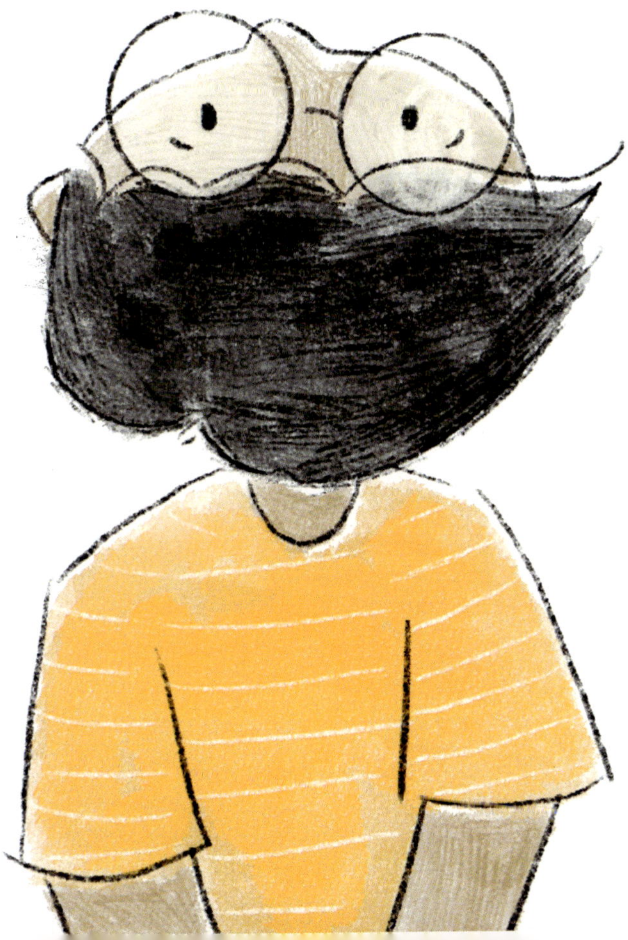

tota books

An imprint of Speaking Tiger Books

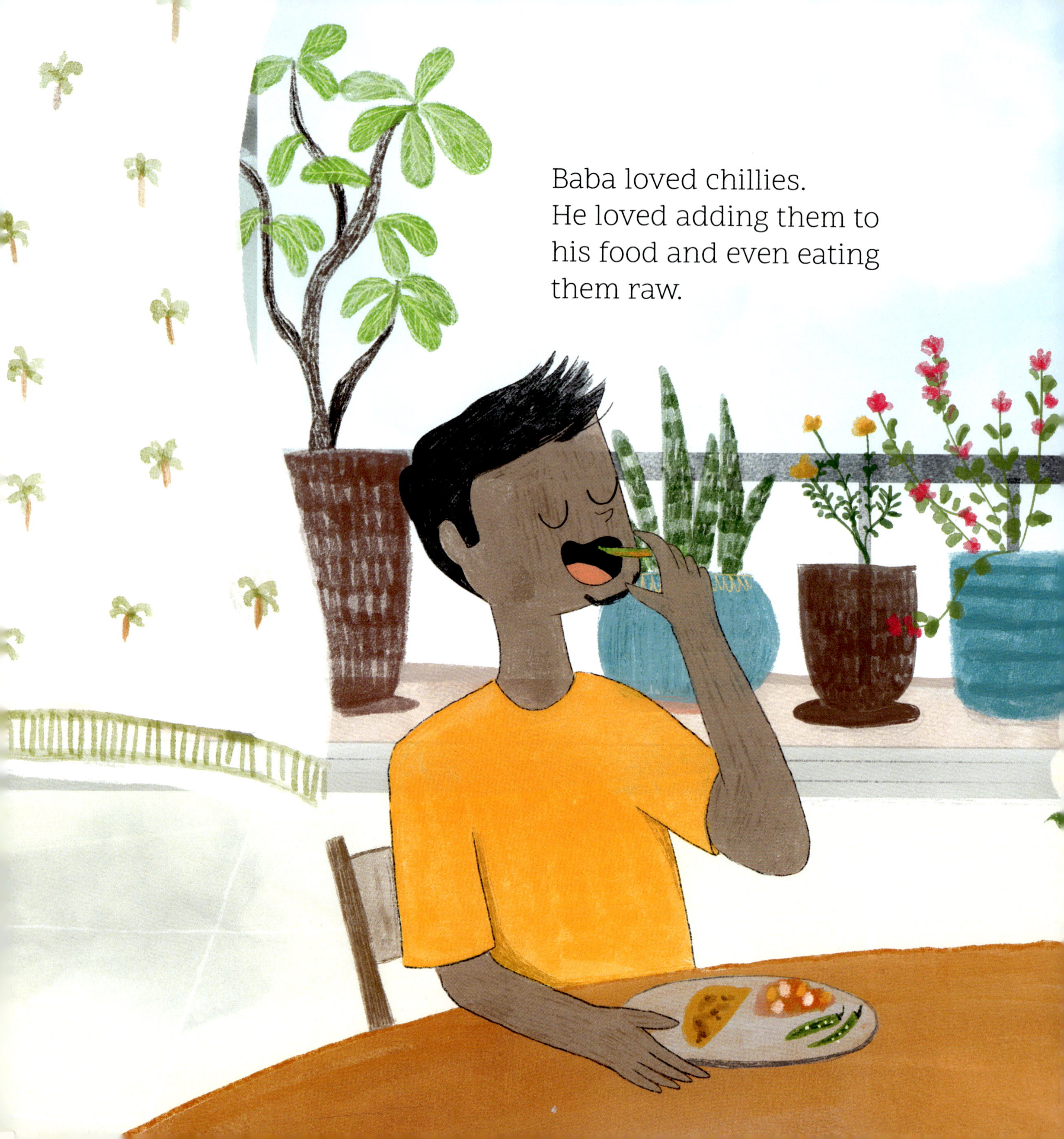

Baba loved chillies.
He loved adding them to
his food and even eating
them raw.

Veer hated chillies.
Ever since he accidently bit into a hot pepper when he was five, he stayed far away from chillies. He would never ever try one, not in his wildest dreams.

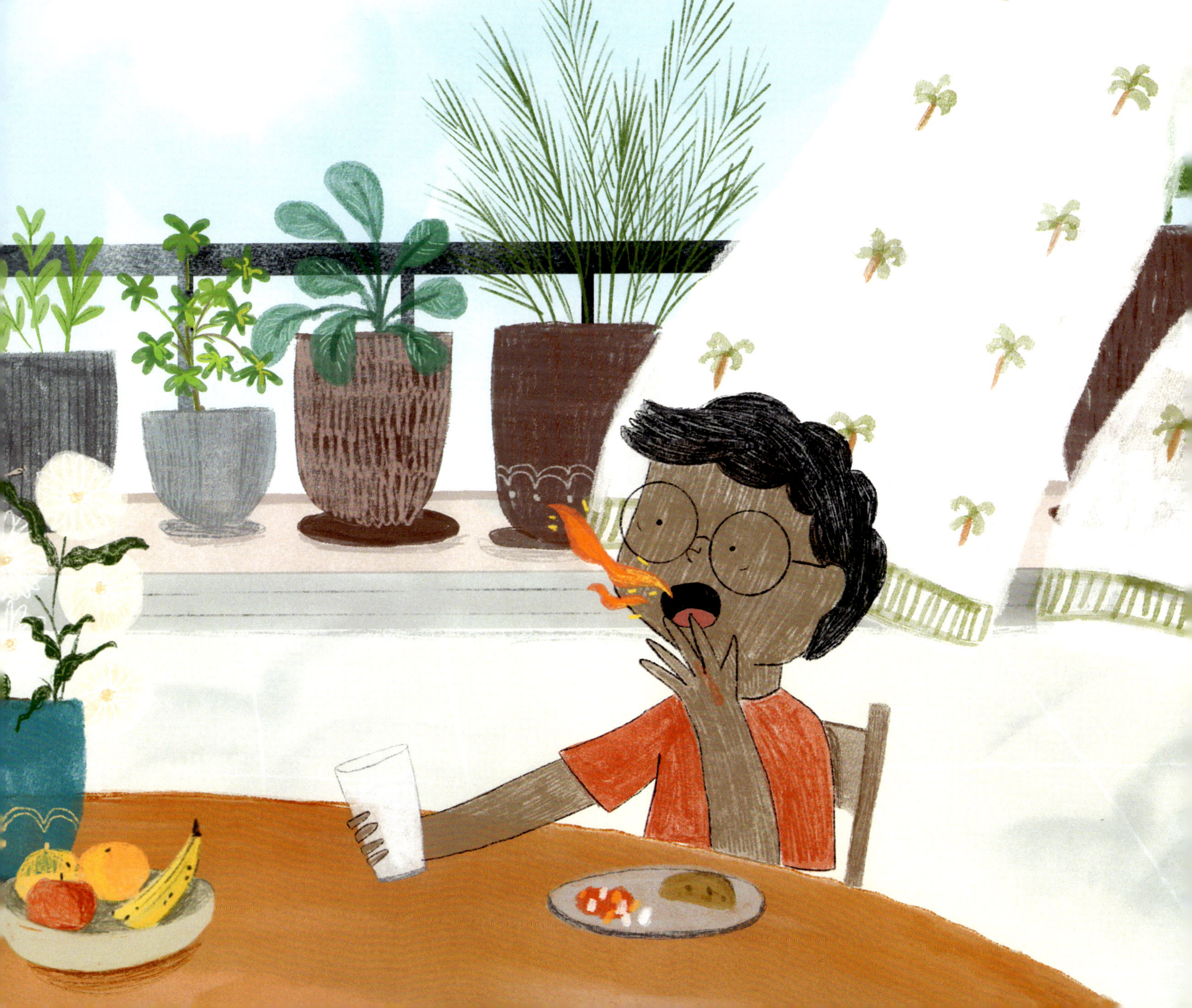

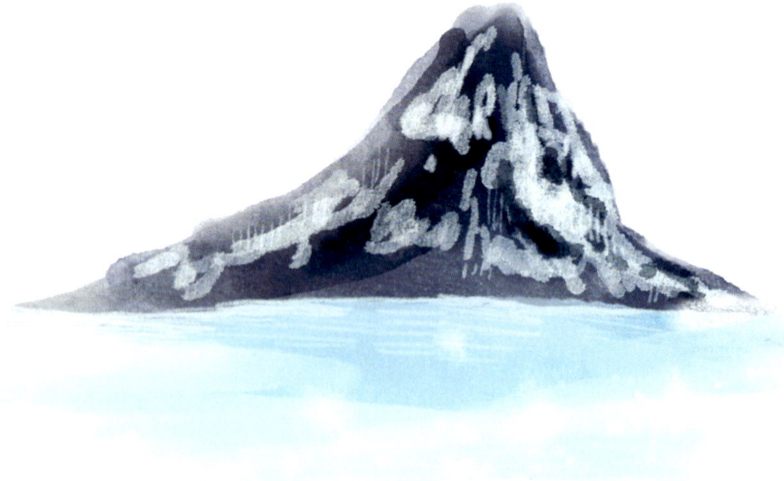

Baba loved collecting chilli seeds from everywhere he went. When Veer and his family visited Sikkim in the holidays, Baba brought back some Dalle chilli seeds.

"But Baba, why do you need to get chilli seeds from everywhere you go?" asked Veer.

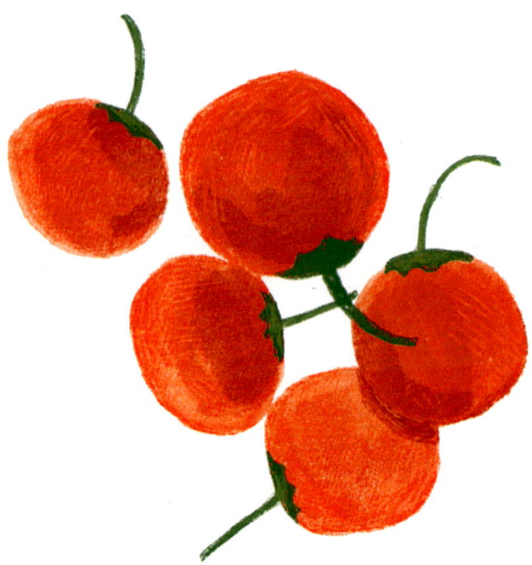

"Because there are many types of chillies in India and the world and each one has its own unique flavour. Some chillies are super spicy and some are not," said Baba, sowing the different variety of chilli seeds in the soil.

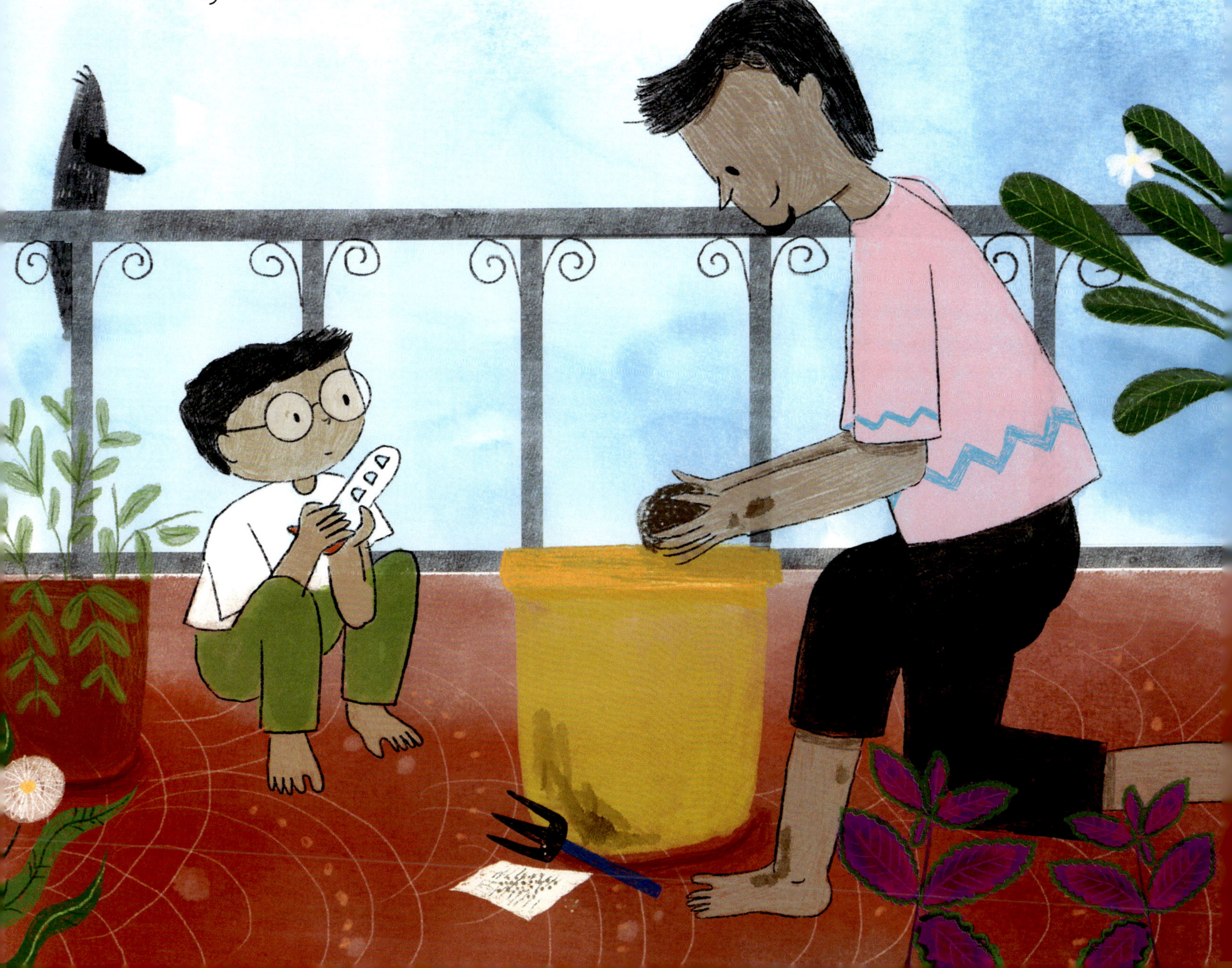

"Infact, we Indians are the kings of spices. We are number one when it comes to eating and growing chillies, even though chillies did not originate here!"

"Really?" asked Veer.

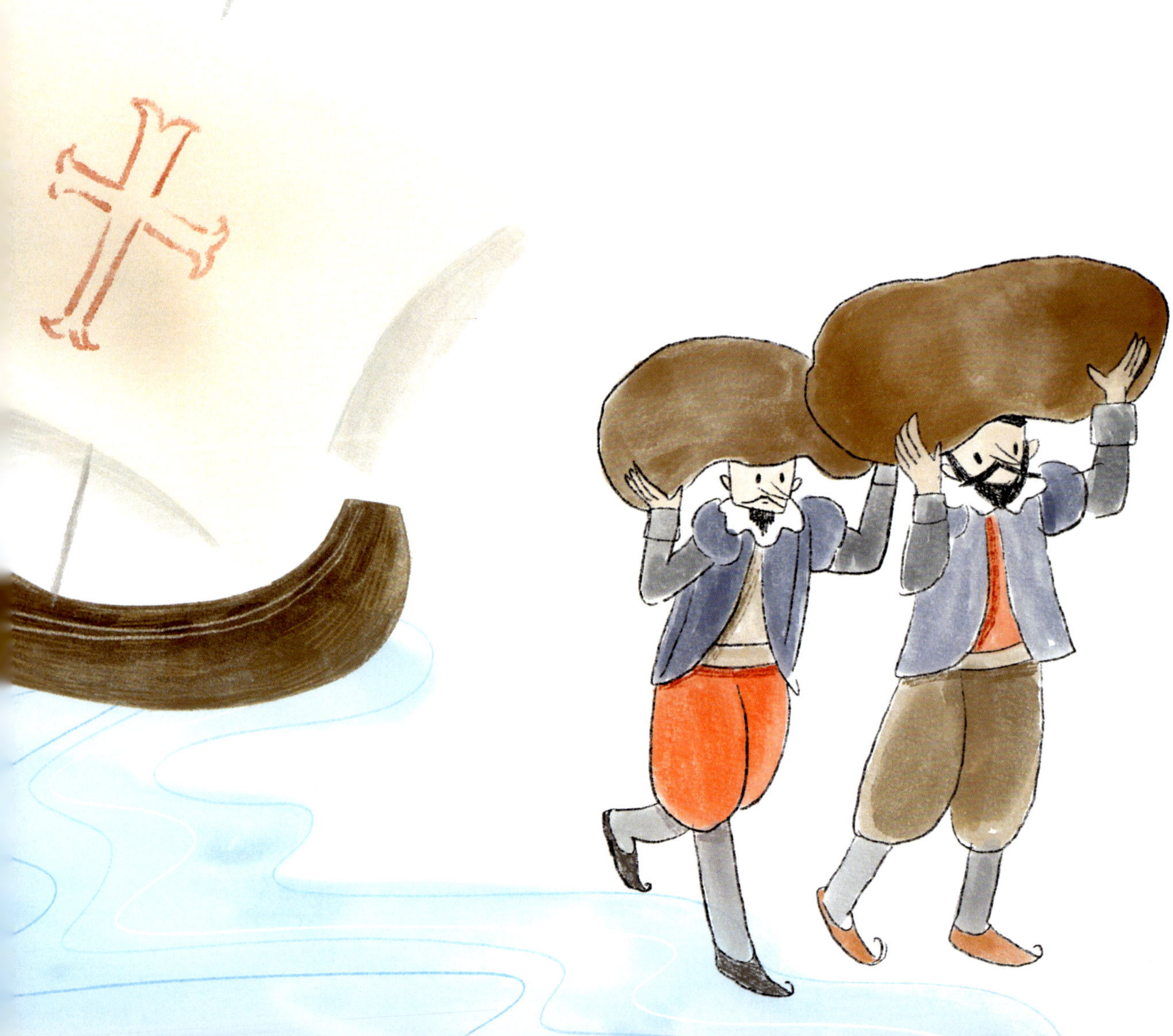

"Yes. Chillies were brought to India a very long time ago, by Vasco-da-Gama and his fleet of Portuguese sailors, all the way from south America."

"Oh, how I wish Vasco-da-Gama didn't bring chillies to India. Then I wouldn't have to eat spicy food," grumbled Veer.

"My dear boy, the Portuguese also brought potato, tomato, corn, papaya, pineapple, guava, chikoo and cashews to India," smiled Baba.

"Oh, I'm very glad about that," gushed Veer.

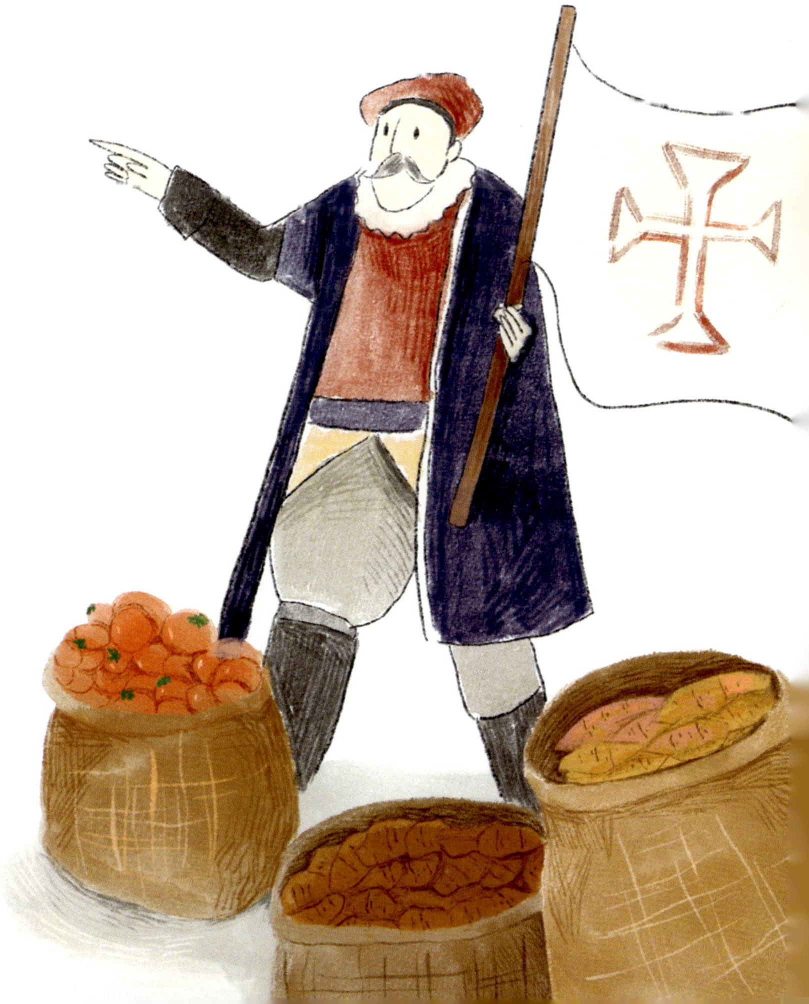

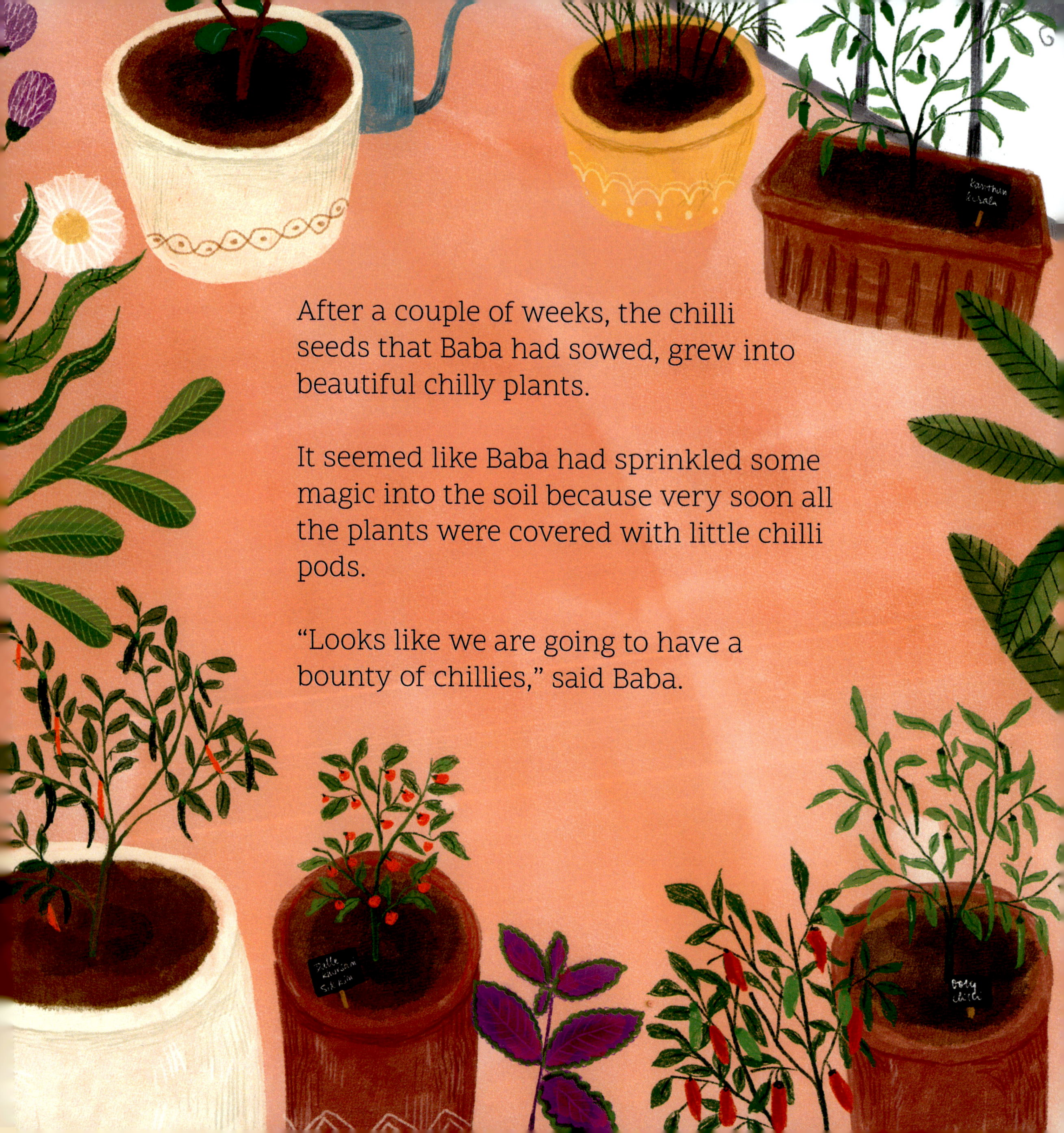

After a couple of weeks, the chilli seeds that Baba had sowed, grew into beautiful chilly plants.

It seemed like Baba had sprinkled some magic into the soil because very soon all the plants were covered with little chilli pods.

"Looks like we are going to have a bounty of chillies," said Baba.

Baba harvested a few and made a red-hot-spicy chutney. Ananya tasted some with her chapati and loved it. Veer did not even touch it.

Veer worried when he saw the chillies grow bigger and bigger.

So many chillies mean super spicy food. He had to do something before the spicy chillies made their way onto his plate.

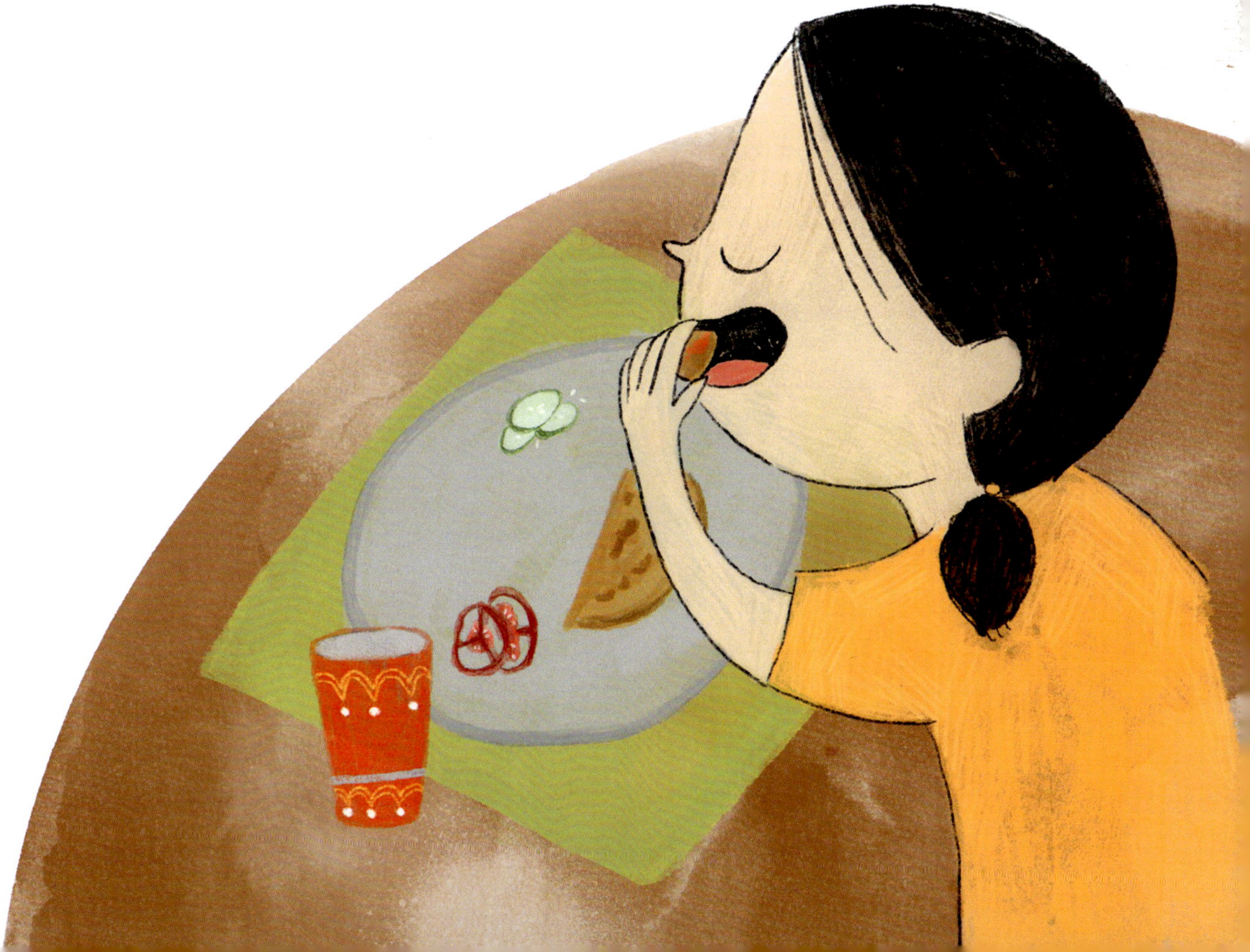

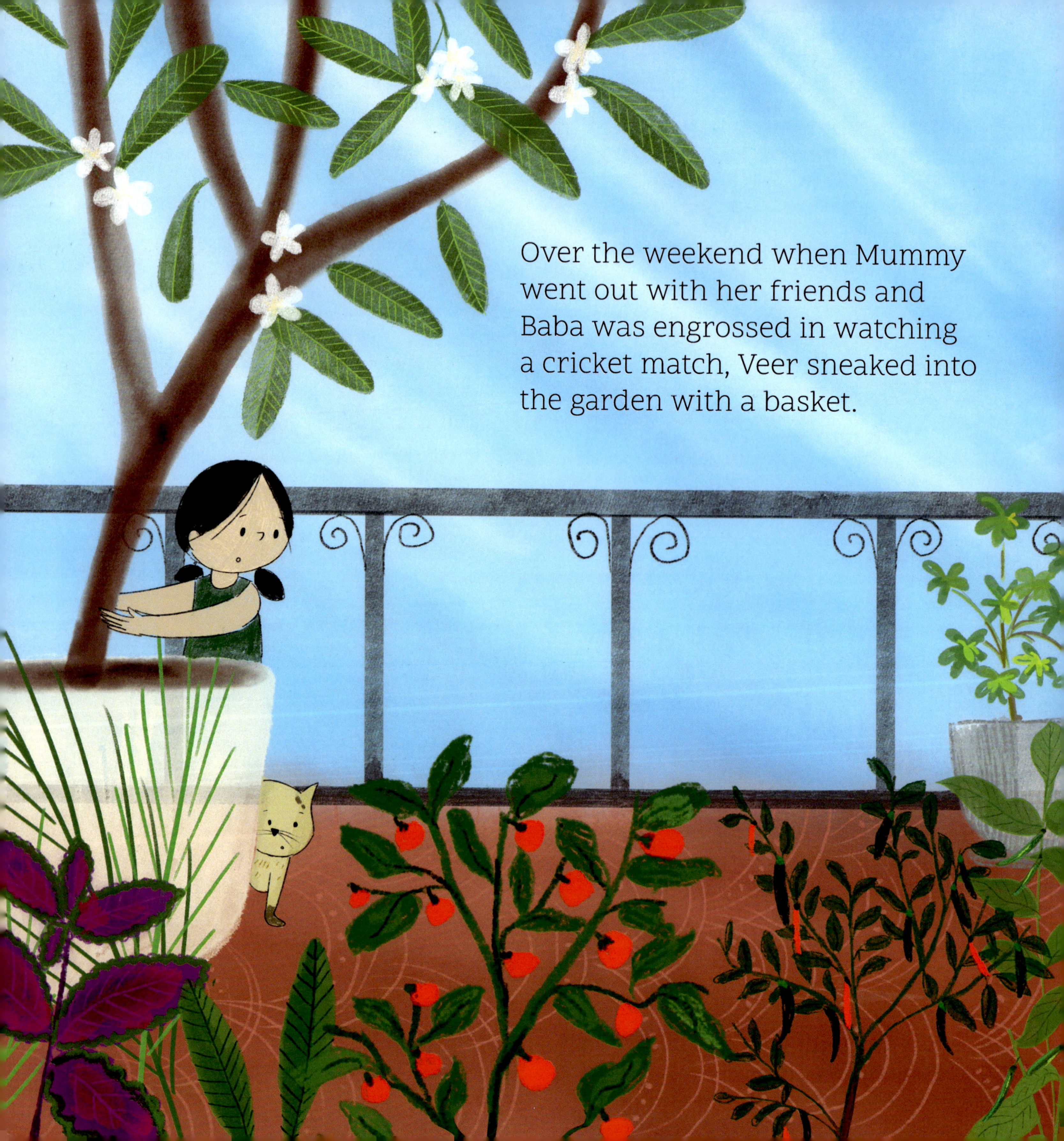

Over the weekend when Mummy went out with her friends and Baba was engrossed in watching a cricket match, Veer sneaked into the garden with a basket.

He quickly plucked all the chillies growing on the different chilli plants… the fat Jalapeños, the huge Ooty chillies, the thin and long Andhra chillies and the round Sikkim chillies. He managed to sneak out with the chillies when no one was looking.

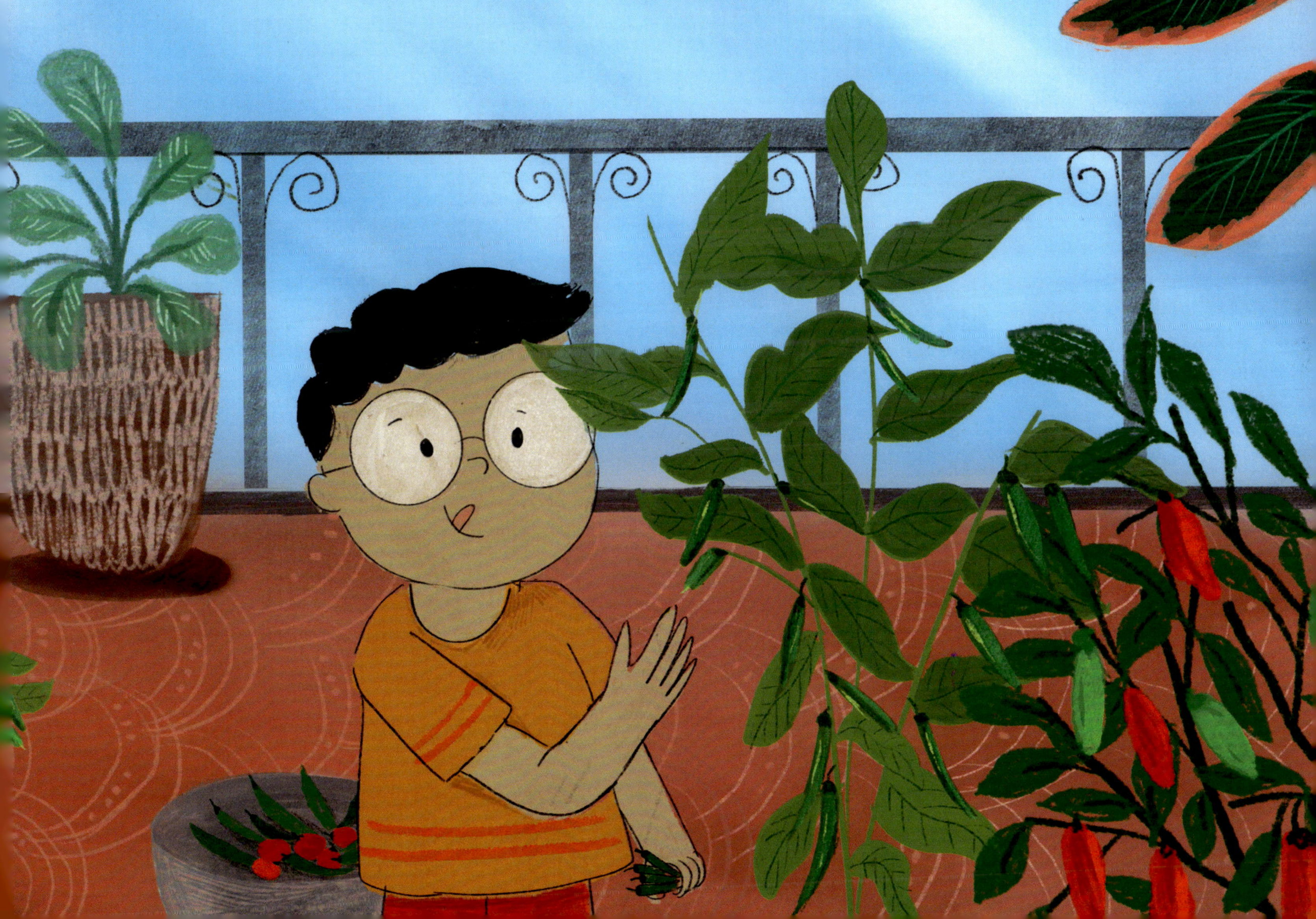

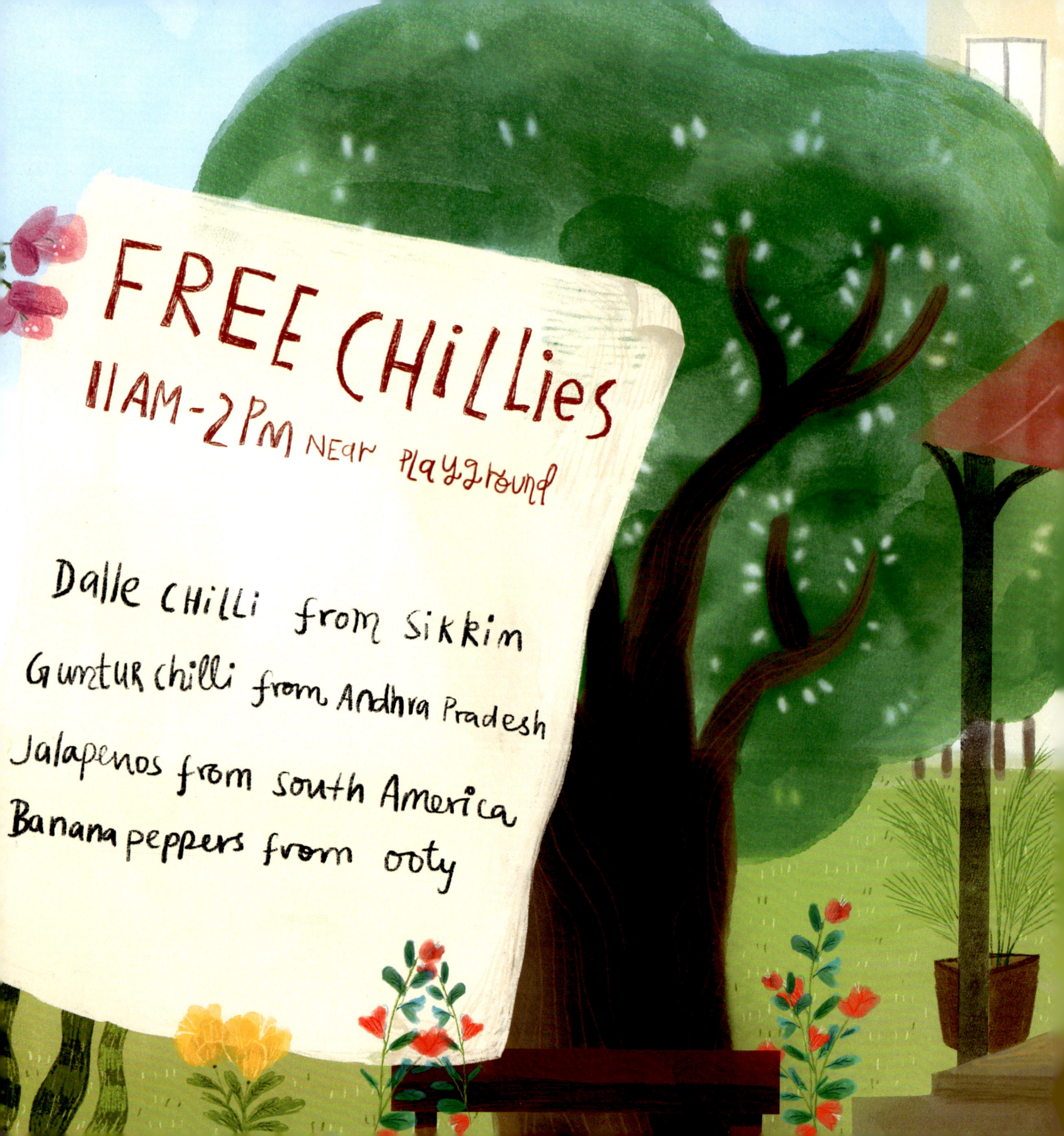
FREE CHiLLies
11AM-2PM NEar PLaygRound
Dalle CHiLLi from Sikkim
GuntUR chilli from Andhra Pradesh
Jalapenos from south America
Banana peppers from ooty

Vaani aunty who was walking her dog noticed the bright poster that Veer had put up.
"Ah! so many varieties of chillies! I wouldn't mind trying some of each."

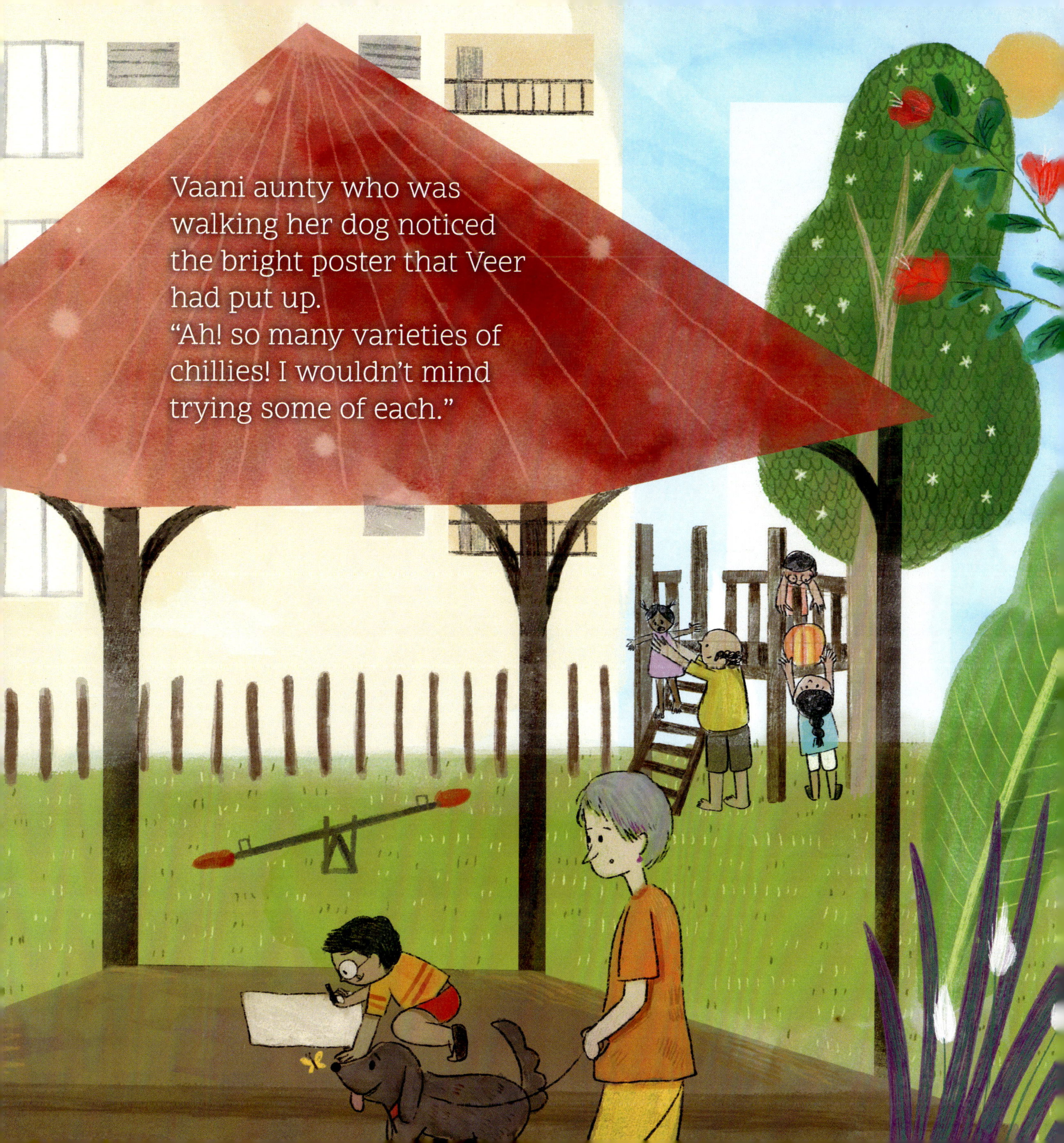

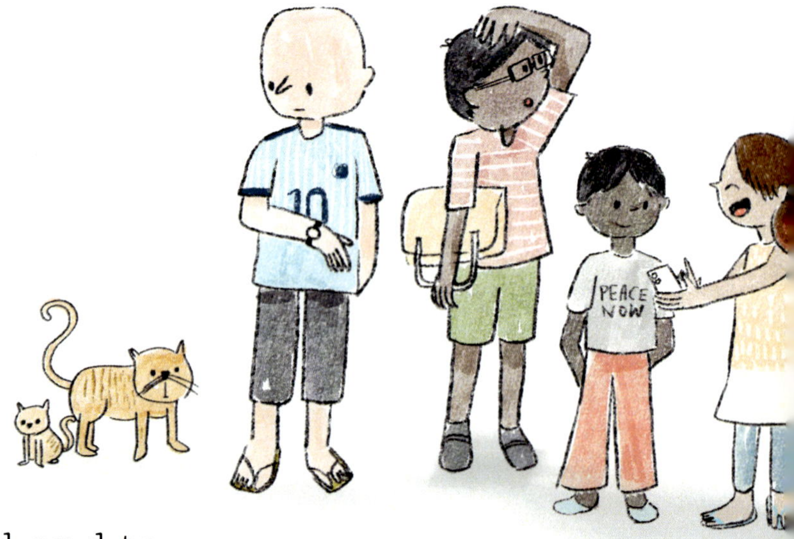


Soon the word spread and to Veer's surprise all the chillies vanished in no time!

"Good riddance," grinned Veer as the last of the chilli lot was handed over to Navin uncle.

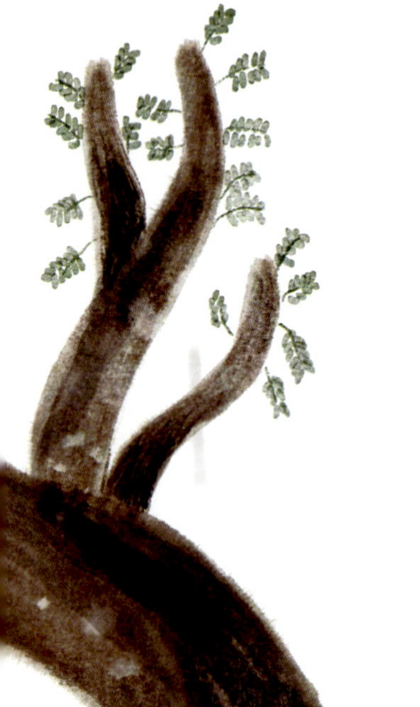

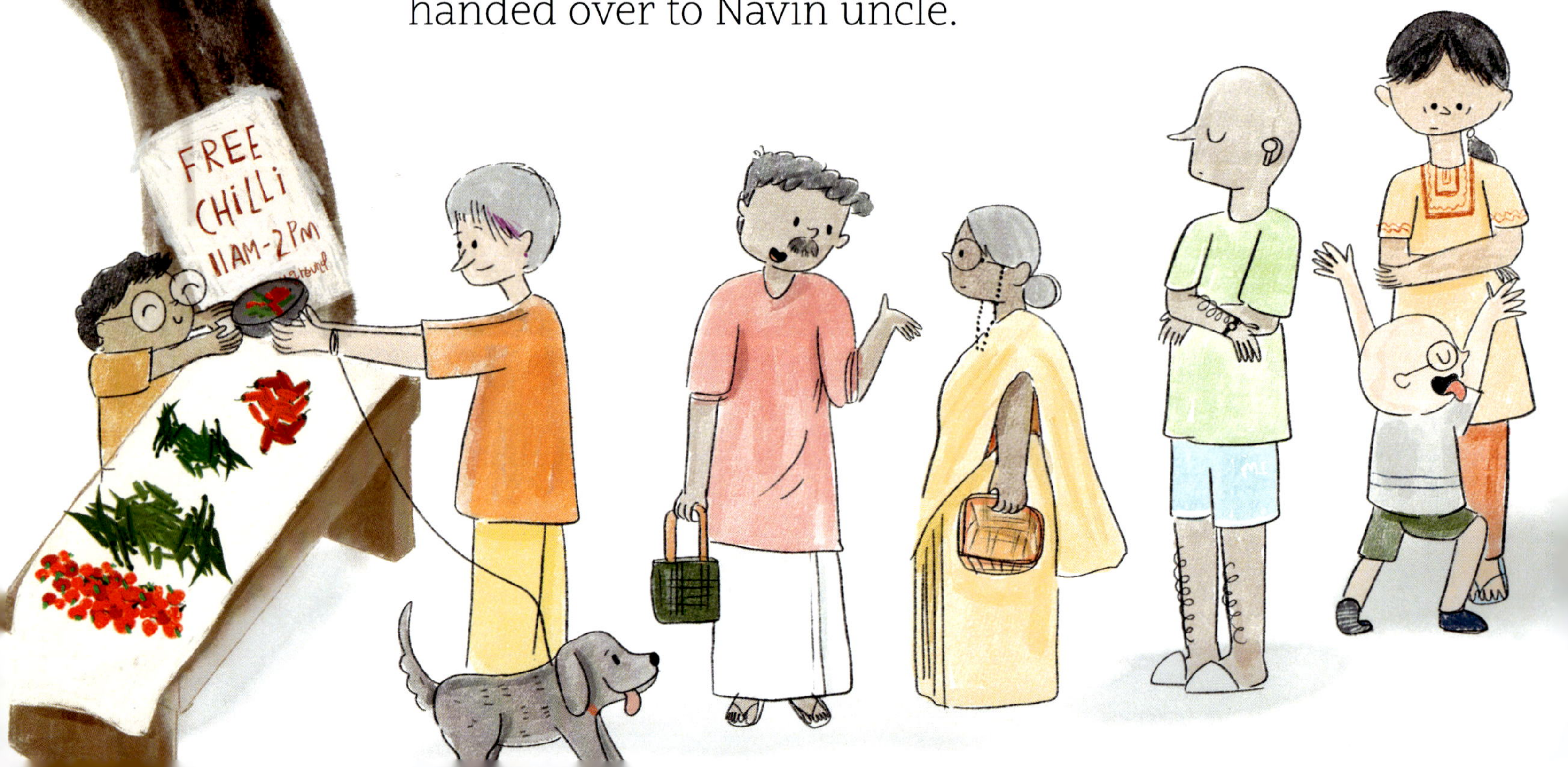

“Where did all my chillies disappear?”
Baba wondered the next day.
Mummy looked equally puzzled.

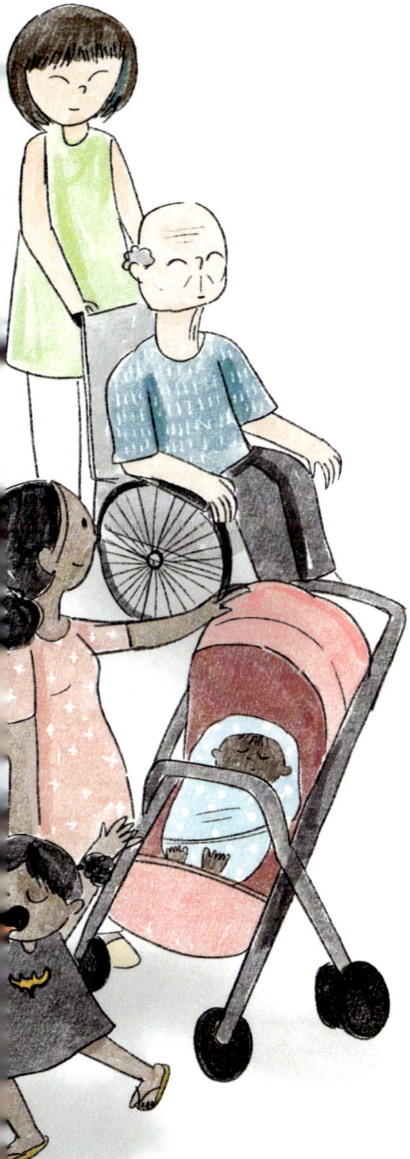

“Maybe the birds and squirrels have developed a taste for chillies,” joked Veer grinning secretly.

He was relieved. “No more spicy food!”

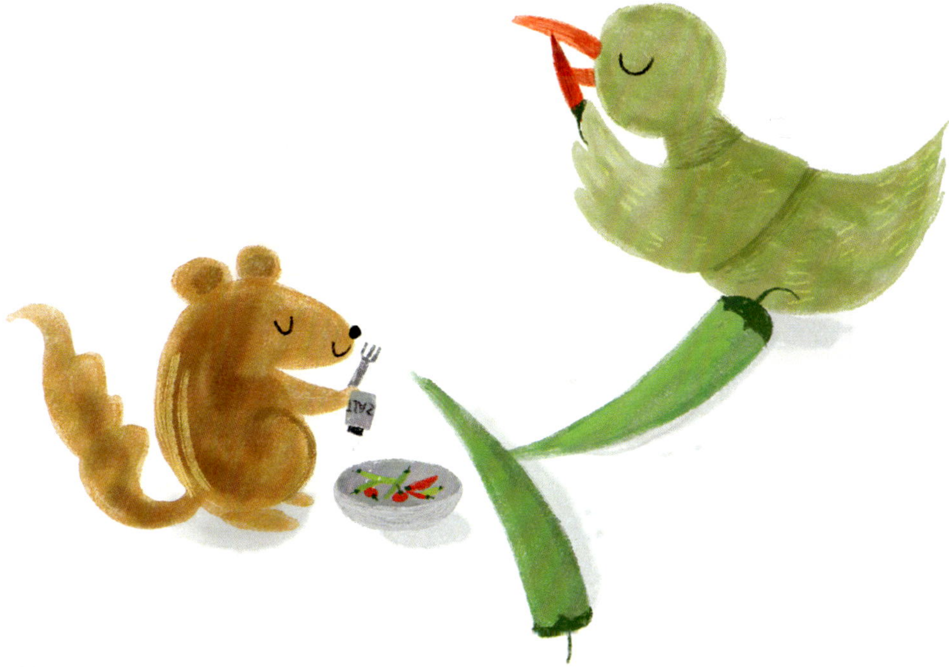

A few days later there was a food festival in the complex. Ananya, Baba and Mummy pestered Veer to come and explore all the delicious home-made food by the resident chefs. Veer reluctantly agreed.

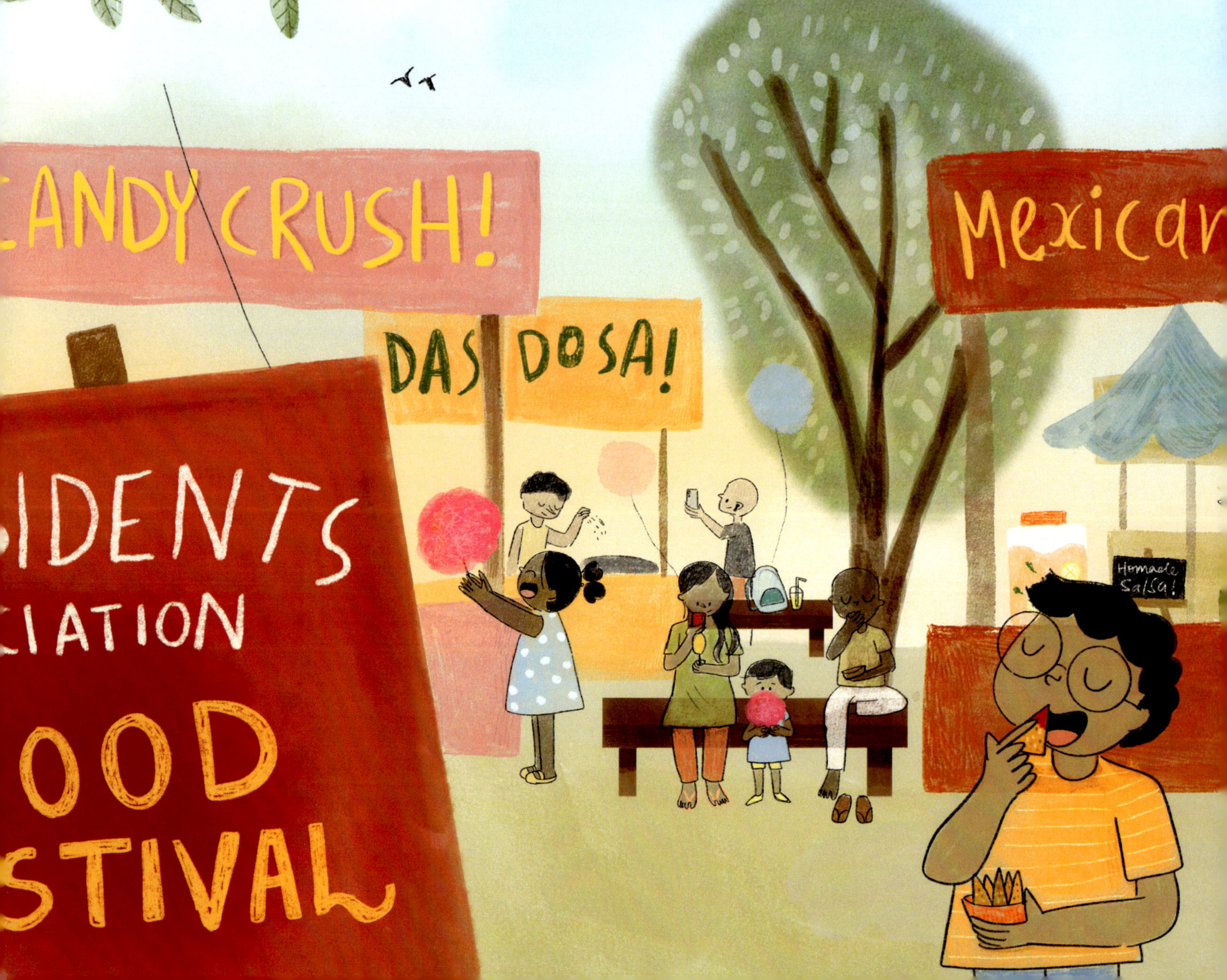

The first stall they visited was Vani Aunty's Mexican delight. Veer dipped some nachos into the salsa and took a bite. His tongue sizzled but he couldn't stop at one. Soon he had licked his plate clean.

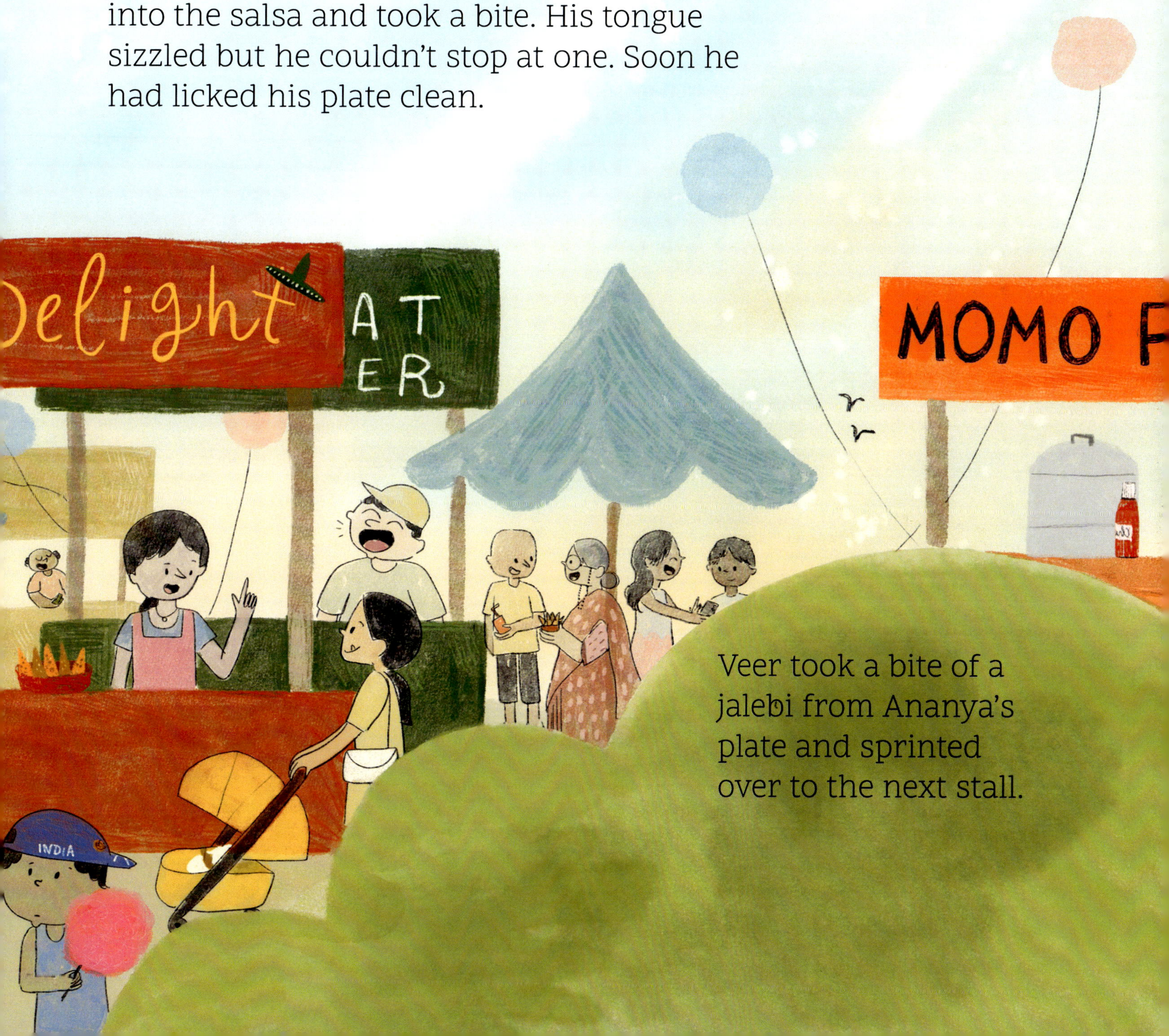


Veer took a bite of a jalebi from Ananya's plate and sprinted over to the next stall.

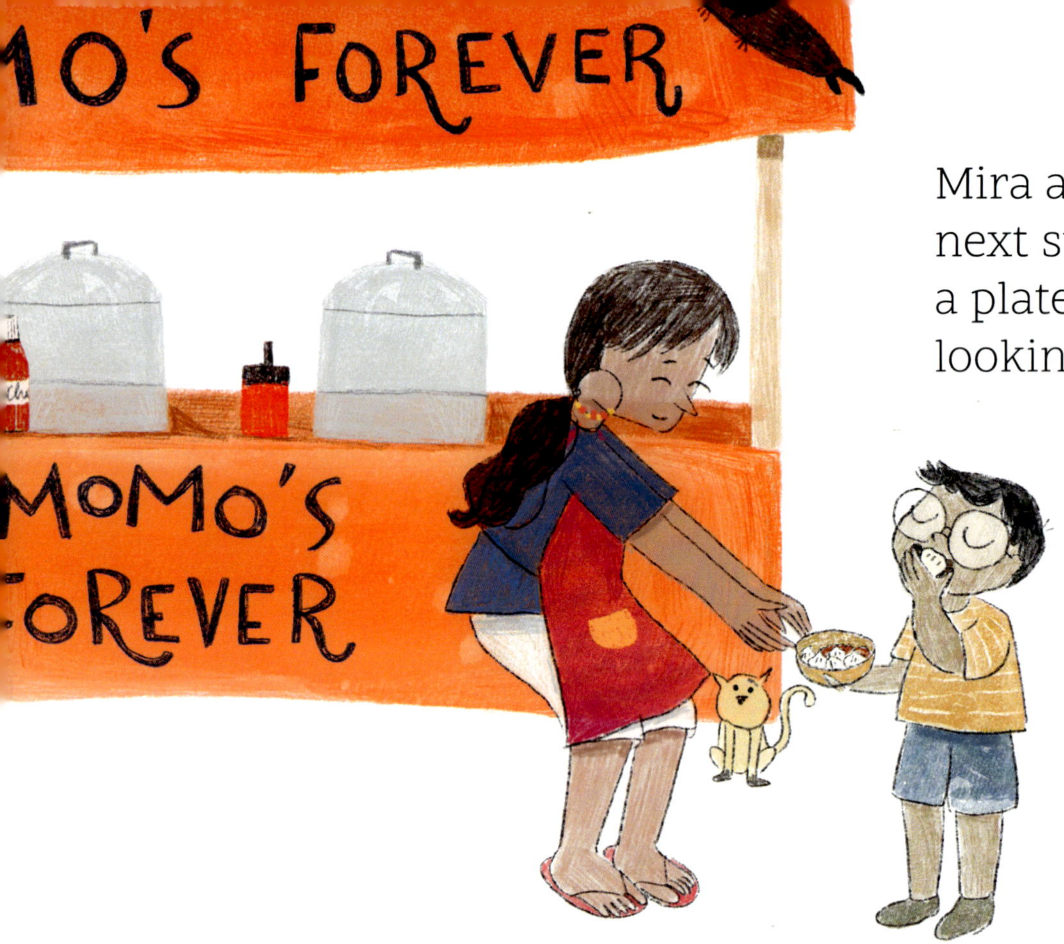


Mira aunty greeted him at the next stall and offered Veer a plate full of scrumptious looking momos. Veer dunked a momo into the red sauce and took a bite. Veer's mouth was on fire but he loved the taste and quickly polished off his plate.

Navin uncle's stall smelled like heaven.

Veer couldn't resist a plate of hot pakoras. He bit into one and then another. His eyes watered but he couldn't stop eating. Soon there were no pakoras left on his plate.

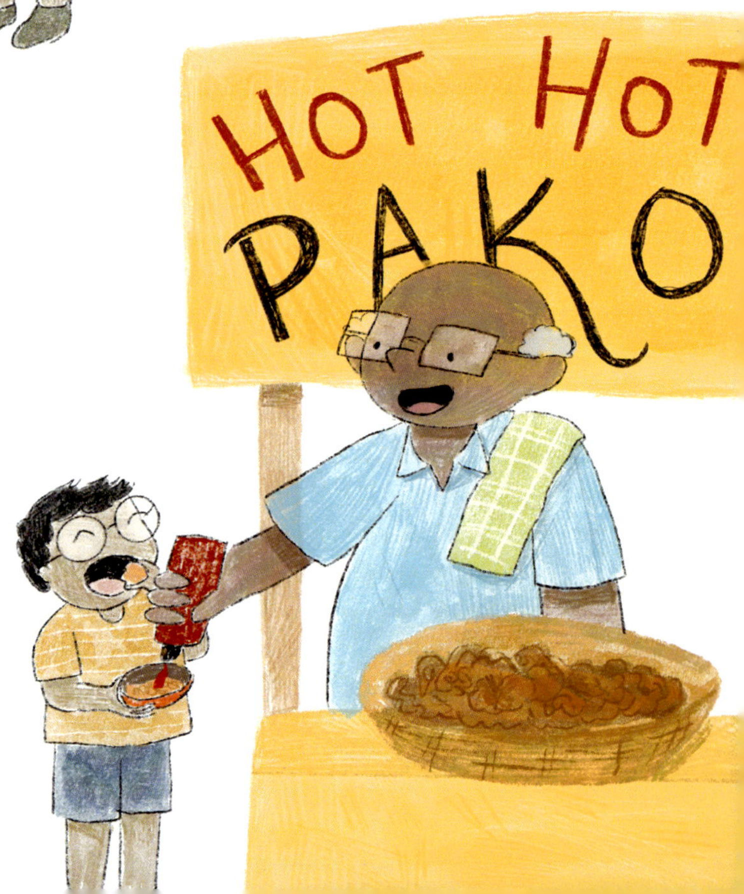

The next stall in line was Gurmeet Aunty's Pickle Mania. There were several pickles on display. "Veer why don't you taste the pickles with some mathri."

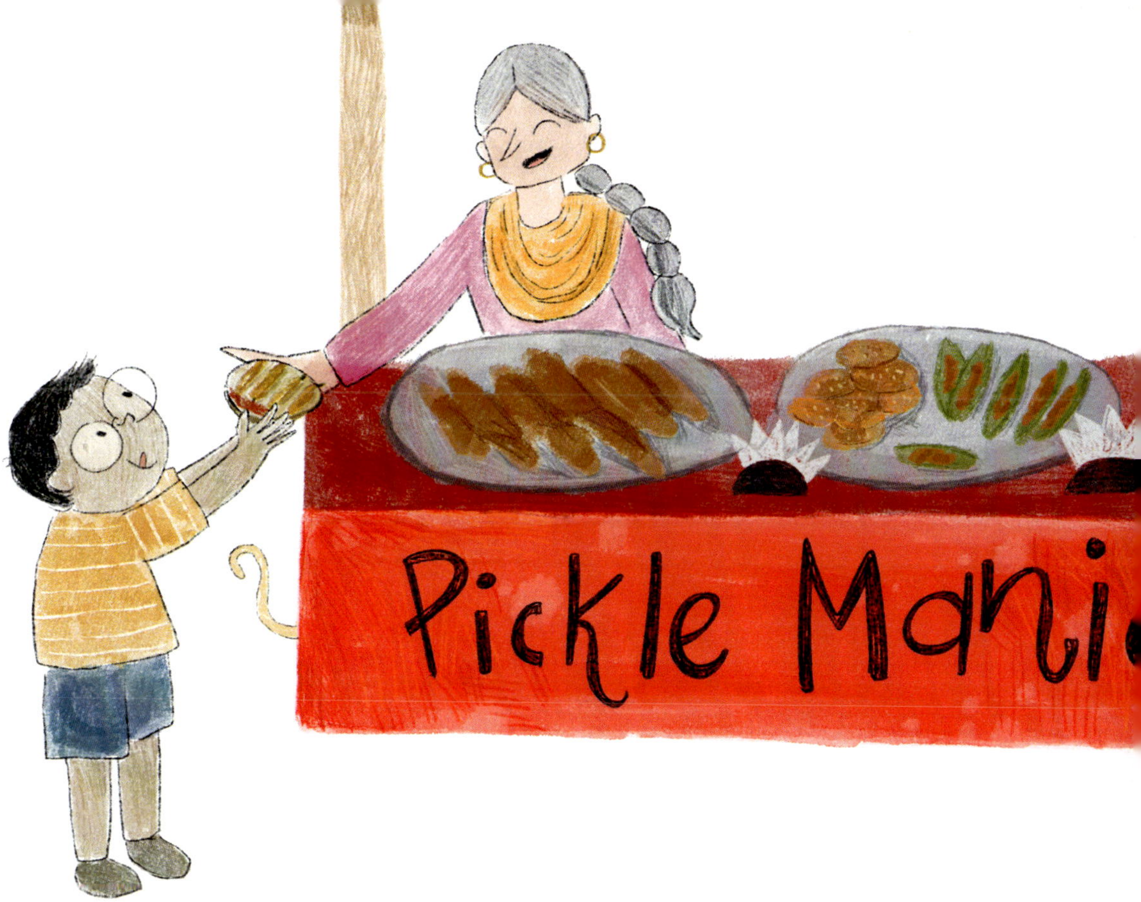


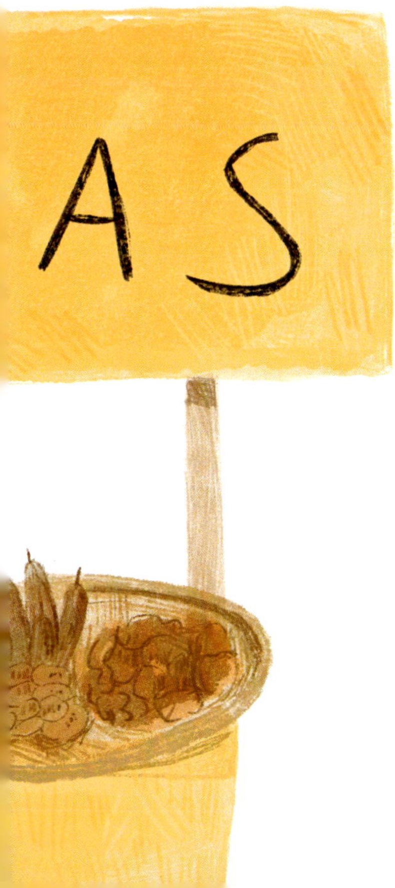


Veer sampled each of the pickles on display. His face turned red but he licked his fingers clean. He even pestered his Mummy to buy some.

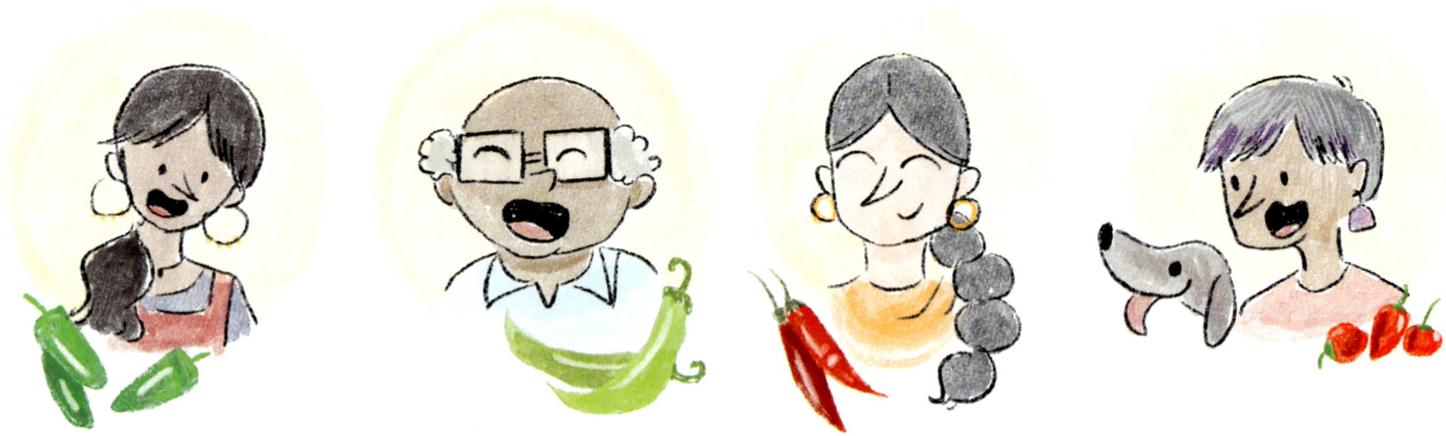

"Veer, the pickles wouldn't have tasted so good if not for the lovely Guntur chillies I got from you last week!" smiled Gurmeet Aunty.
"Thank you for being so kind and sharing them!"
Veer's face turned red like the chillies in the pickle.

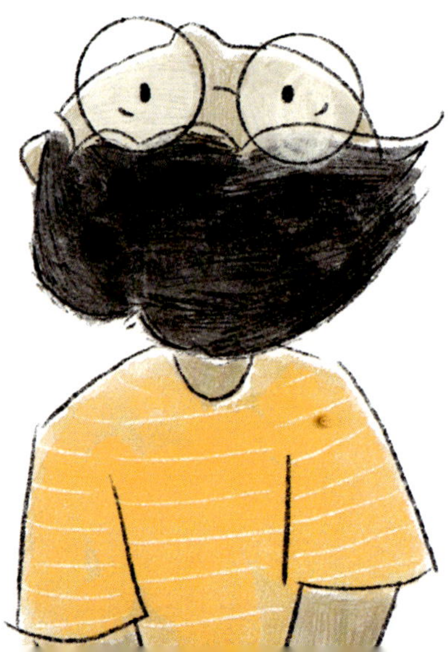

"Veer guess what, the pakoras you just relished were made with the Ooty peppers you so generously distributed," laughed Navin uncle.

"And I'm so glad you loved the momos Veer dear, after all the delicious sauce is made with the Dalle chillies you gave me," smiled Mira aunty.

"Veer, guess what! I made the salsa with the Jalapeños you gave me," said Vani aunty. "They were just perfect!"

Veer looked around sheepishly. His little secret had tumbled out of the bag! Veer's parents looked at each other and smiled. Ananya giggled.

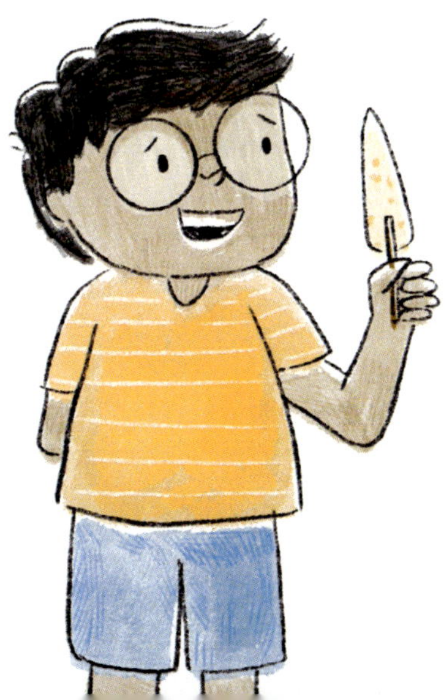

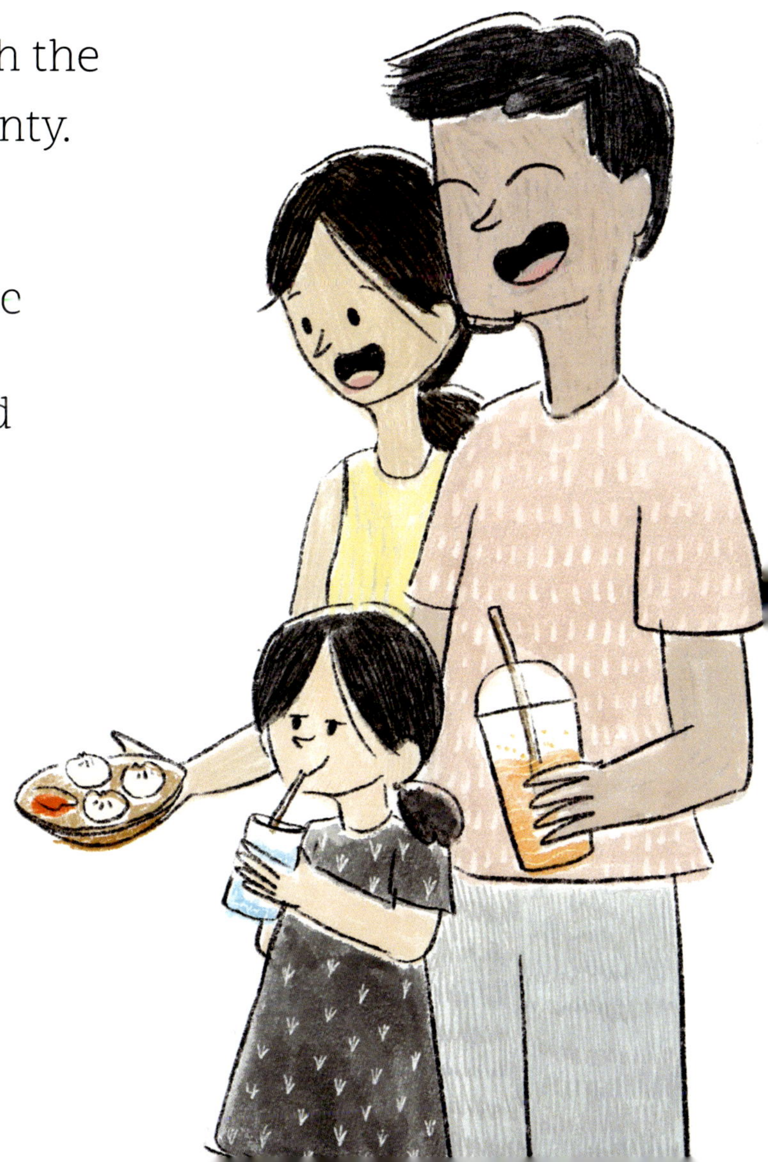

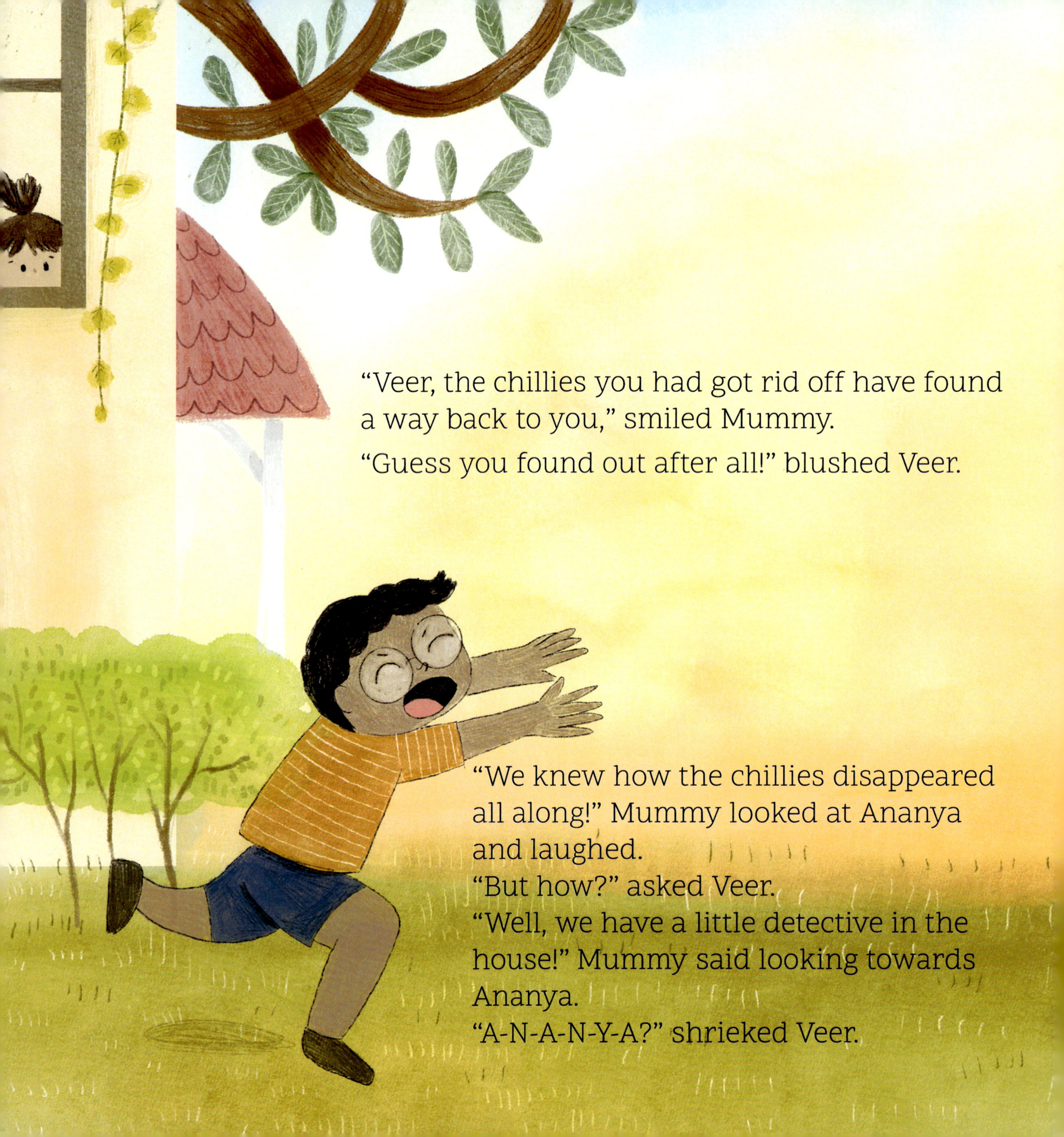

"Veer, the chillies you had got rid off have found a way back to you," smiled Mummy.

"Guess you found out after all!" blushed Veer.

"We knew how the chillies disappeared all along!" Mummy looked at Ananya and laughed.
"But how?" asked Veer.
"Well, we have a little detective in the house!" Mummy said looking towards Ananya.
"A-N-A-N-Y-A?" shrieked Veer.

“At least I made you come to the food fair to taste all the chillies, Bhaiya!” Ananya grinned. “Didn’t you enjoy all the food made with the lovely chillies Baba grew?”

“Yes, I did,” admitted Veer. “Chillies aren’t as bad as I thought!”

“Can I have another helping of the nachos and salsa please?”

“Ofcourse you can,” smiled Vani aunty.

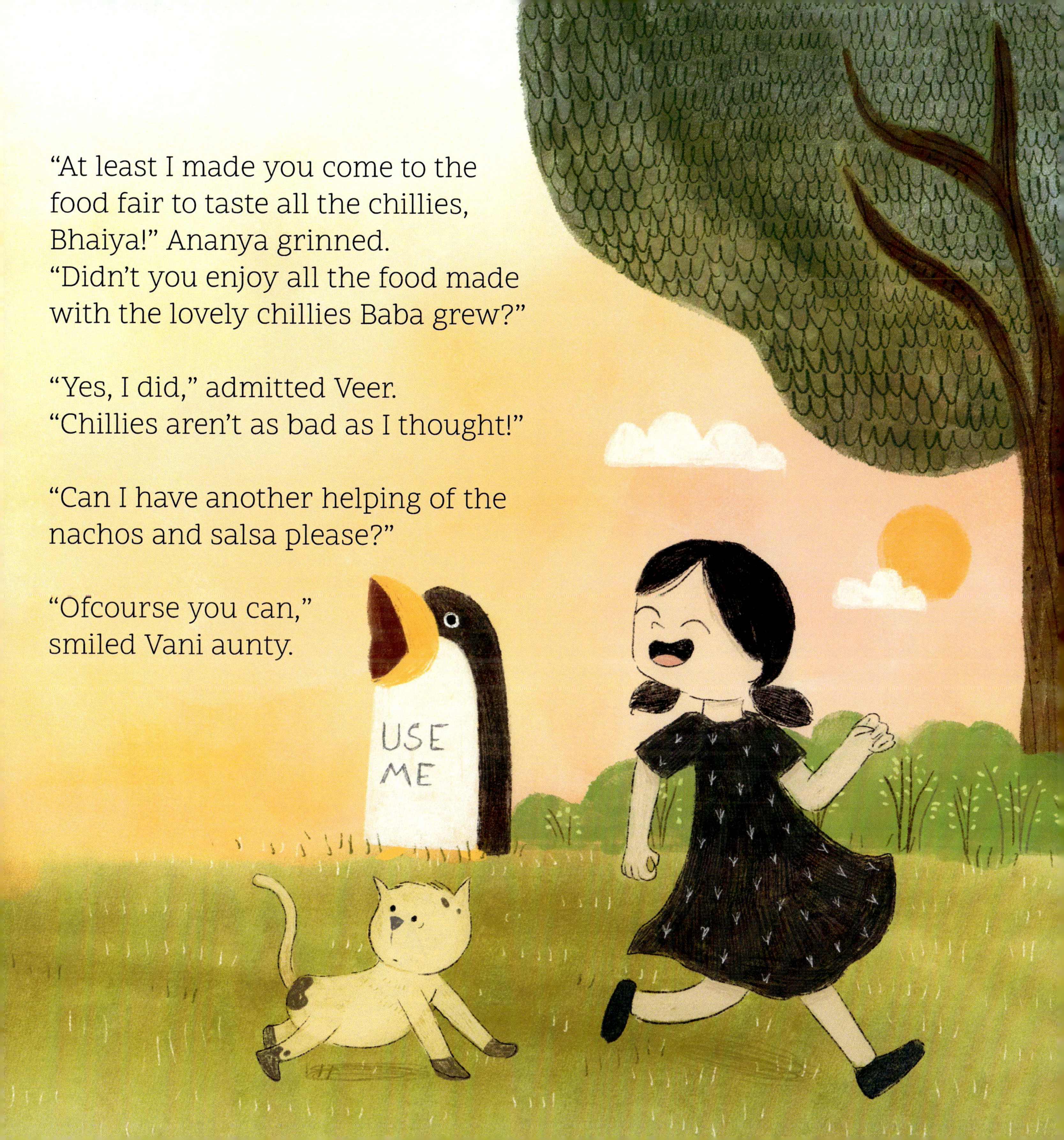

"Glad you discovered the taste of chillies," said Mummy. "Without chillies our food would be so bland and boring!"

"A bit of chilly makes the food come alive,
A bit of chilly I do not mind," laughed Veer as he licked the spicy salsa off his fingers.

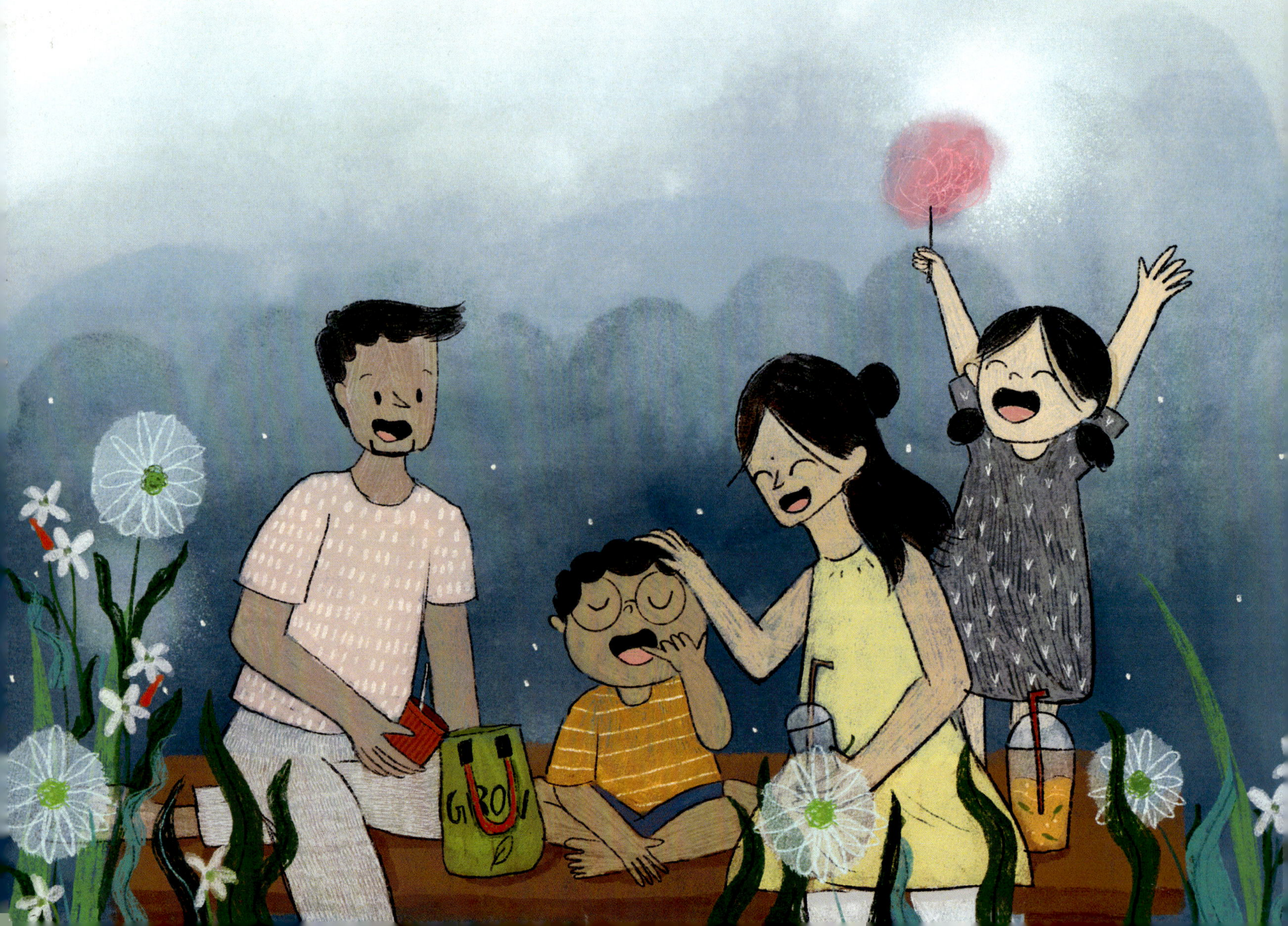